Philosophical Thinking is Yoga for the Mind®

Also available from Upper West Side Philosophers, Inc.:

~

November Rose: A Speech on Death
by Kathrin Stengel
(Independent Publisher Book Award 2008)

November Rose: Eine Rede über den Tod
by Kathrin Stengel

Philosophical Fragments of a Contemporary Life
by Julien David

17 Vorurteile, die wir Deutschen gegen Amerika und die Amerikaner haben und die so nicht ganz stimmen können
by Misha Waiman

Descartes' Devil: Three Meditations
by Durs Grünbein

Upper West Side Philosophers, Inc. provides a publication venue for original philosophical thinking steeped in lived life, in line with our motto: *philosophical living & lived philosophy*.

PRAISE

for

THE DNA OF PREJUDICE

*

"This remarkable book takes the reader through the many layers of meaning that accompany the word 'prejudice'. By critically confronting the ways in which we think and speak about prejudice, Michael Eskin clears the path for a new understanding of prejudice as a concept, a phenomenon, and a lived experience. Combining analytical rigor with sound practical suggestions, this book speaks to a broad audience and will serve as a valuable companion for anyone who shares the author's passionate commitment to confronting and eradicating prejudice."

LICIA CARLSON, Harvard University, author of *The Faces of Intellectual Disability: Philosophical Reflections*

*

"An original, much needed (and overdue) philosophical work with important practical and political implications, not only for our own societies, but also for those who work cross-culturally, like diplomats. We encounter the issues Michael Eskin discusses in one form or another often—it seems like every day."

MATTHEW G. BOYSE, United States Consul General

*

"Sedulously argued, this thoughtful book attempts nothing less than a revalorization of prejudice—its meaning, the way it manifests itself, and its effect on individuals (the prejudiced and those who feel the sting of it) as well as the world around them. It's an ambitious undertaking, deftly navigated by Michael Eskin, who cogently offers an entirely original framework for identifying prejudice and confronting it. In an environment that has been optimistically (if naively) called post-racial—in which racial, gender, and ethnic divides appear to have as much poignant resolve as ever—Eskin's important book offers a set of powerful pathways for comprehending and addressing a pernicious aspect of life that remains far too at home in the headlines, the rural backroads, and the chill of urban streets."

JEFFREY ROTHFEDER, former BusinessWeek, Time Inc., and Bloomberg News editor, and author of *McIlhenny's Gold: How a Louisiana Family Built the Tabasco Empire* and *Every Drop for Sale: Our Desperate Battle over Water in a World About to Run Out*

*

"... a wonderful essay that excels both at analyzing the essence of prejudice and at providing a demonstration of the practice of philosophical thinking accessible to all with no requirement or knowledge of the history of philosophy. Highly recommended for all who have an interest in the topic of prejudice and/or philosophical thinking."

JEAN-PAUL SCHMETZ, CEO, 10betterpages, Cliqz.com, Schmetzfunds

The DNA *of* PREJUDICE

~

On the One and the Many

MICHAEL ESKIN

Upper West Side Philosophers, Inc.

New York • 2010

Published by Upper West Side Philosophers, Inc.
P. O. Box 250645, New York, NY 10025, USA
www.westside-philosophers.com

Cover images: Russian Jews in forced labor, Mogilev, Belarus, July 1941; photograph by Rudolf Kessler; courtesy of the German Federal Archive, image 101I-138-1083-27; Omaha courthouse lynching ("Burning of Will Brown's Body") Sept. 28, 1919; courtesy of the Omaha World-Herald; Émilie du Châtelet (1706-1749), detail of a portrait by an unknown French artist.

Library of Congress Control Number: 2009933722
ISBN-13: 978-0-9795829-5-0 (pbk.)
ISBN-10: 0-9795829-5-4 (pbk.)

Typesetting and Design: Upper West Side Philosophers, Inc.
Printed by Offset Impressions, Inc., Reading, PA
Printed in the United States of America

CONTENTS

~

"… how pernicious it is to implant prejudices: they will eventually revenge themselves upon their authors or on their authors' descendants."

IMMANUEL KANT

~

"... deep-seated prejudice is stronger by far than the most convincing evidence to the contrary …"

EDMUND HUSSERL

~

"A misguided 'love of simplicity', David Hume remarks, 'has been the source of much false reasoning'.—Sometimes, keeping it simple will actually complicate things. The trick is to make it simple without simplifying it."

JULIEN DAVID

PREFATORY NOTE

~

In writing this book, it has been my goal to think through and sort out one particular pattern of sloppy thinking found across our culture—our cavalier understanding and application of the term 'prejudice' —and to offer a conceptual guide on how to avoid the pitfalls of such sloppy thinking and its deleterious consequences. Think of this book, then, as a handbook or manual intended for concrete, real-life use.

~

Several readers have asked me whether I think that prejudice is only directed at people, or whether it can also be directed at animals and things (including material objects, qualities, character traits etc.). In the case of animals, it seems to me, the answer is clearly yes. In the case of things, the situation is slightly more complicated; however, here as well, I believe, the answer ought to be yes, especially insofar as, when it comes to prejudice, things are frequently taken metonymically to stand in for those who make them or those who have them. Think, for instance, of fellow Americans who, on principle, dislike *foreign* cars despite the fact that some of them, Japanese or German cars, say, have been proven to outperform their domestic counterparts. Clearly, the issue here seems less cars *per se* than the *foreigners* who build them and their putative characteristics in the minds of those Americans who dislike their products (in the case of Japanese and Germans, in particular, more or less explicit xenophobia is compounded by the memory of Pearl Harbor, D-Day, the Holocaust etc.).

In order not unduly to curtail the referential purview of 'prejudice', I have endeavored, throughout this book, to use the term 'object' (and, less frequently, 'target' or 'entity') to refer to whomever or whatever prejudice may be directed at in the most general sense (leaving it up to you to flesh it out more concretely in any given instance depending on your personal history, background, profession, horizon of associations, or simply whatever might be going on in your life). Thus, when I speak of the "object of prejudice" or "the object prejudice happens to be directed at," for instance, it should be understood that 'object' covers any 'living being' or 'thing'.

Only in those instances in which using 'object' or 'target' would have either been stylistically awkward or distorted the sense (as in the numerous definitions of 'prejudice' that I provide), do I speak of "someone or something" as the object of prejudice. Here as well, however, it should be understood that 'someone' includes any 'living being'.

THE DNA *of* PREJUDICE

ON THE ONE AND THE MANY

1

THE PERSISTENCE OF PREJUDICE

~

Prejudice is ubiquitous. Our lives are rife with it. Wherever we go, we are likely to encounter it in its manifold guises. Ever ready to hand, it feeds into our proclivity to explain away the complexities, subtleties, and specificities of personality, culture, and the world at large in the name of simplification, abstraction, and generalization. Prejudice knows no social or economic boundaries. It is equally prevalent among the poor and the rich, the educated and the uneducated, the rank-and-file and the elite. Immigrant and native, tourist and anthropologist are equally vulnerable to its insidious and pernicious charms. It has no redeeming features, causing harm wherever it treads: to its object, by reducing it to a handful of—typically, undesirable—traits, thereby setting it up for contempt, ridicule, hatred, and violence; to the one who holds it, by imprisoning him within the walls of its own making, by shutting him off from reality, by filling him with ill will and, all too often, hostility toward others, thereby impoverishing and poisoning his existence and, in the worst case, turning him into a criminal.

Why does prejudice have such a strong hold on us? Why is it so persistent, so difficult—if not to say, virtually impossible—to eradicate?

Many an attempt has been made at explaining the persistence of prejudice in etiological, psychological, behavioral, and socio-historical terms. An extensive body of knowledge on prejudice in its many forms has been amassed predicated on such questions as: How does prejudice come into being and under what conditions? Which individuals or groups hold what kinds of prejudice, and to what extent can the incidence of prejudice be said to be a function of education, economic status, socialization, acculturation, as well as historical and political pressures and constraints? What are the emotional and psychological springs of prejudice, and what needs does it fulfill for the individual or the group?[1]

One would think that with this body of knowledge concerning the conditions and manifestations of prejudice in hand we would be further along on the arduous road to its demise. Yet if we look around us, we cannot fail to observe that prejudice is rampant.[2] Thus, it would seem that, at best, a tenuous —if not wholly fortuitous—connection can plausibly be established between understanding, or presuming to understand, the individual and collective origins as well as the psychological and socio-historical conditions of prejudice and the rate of its *de facto* decline. Often, the same people who presume to understand so well the underlying conditions of *others'* prejudice (and ought thus *a fortiori* to be able to apply this knowledge to themselves) tend to be blind to their own bigotry. Often, the ostensible overcoming of prejudice on the part of members of one group against members of another group will be accompanied by the rise among members of the same group of similar prejudice directed elsewhere. Often, the same people who oppose prejudice in one context will themselves act prejudicially in another. In other words, prejudice tends to get displaced rather than disappear. Concomitantly, the possession of pertinent *facts* or *data* doesn't entail the demise of prejudice either. For instance, knowing that the majority of contemporary Germans do not subscribe to National Socialist ideology has not made the prejudice go away among some that 'deep down' Germans 'somehow' continue to be Nazis.

Why is this? Could it be that something about prejudice has escaped traditional approaches to it? Something that needs to be accounted for first if we want more fully to grasp the staying power of prejudice, which, in turn, is a precondition for reining it in and, ideally, overcoming it? My answer is yes. And this 'something' is, I believe, nothing less than the very *meaning* of 'prejudice' at its most basic level—at the level of its 'molecular' structure, its 'DNA', as it were—which, as I shall demonstrate, turns out to be much more complex and intricate than both dictionary and common knowledge would allow for, and which holds the key to understanding what makes prejudice so persistent and tenacious *in its very essence*, and where and how best to begin tackling it with a view to rendering it powerless.

2

THE 'PICKLER INCIDENT'

~

Last year, I traveled to Germany under the auspices of the US Consulate General in connection with a short book I had published entitled *17 Prejudices That We Germans Hold Against America and Americans and That Can't Quite Be True.*[1] I had been invited to deliver several public lectures on the subject of my book at various local academic institutions and give a workshop at the US Consulate General in Düsseldorf, Germany, geared specifically toward US and German consular officials, politicians, and cultural representatives at large on how productively to deal with and avoid the pitfalls of cultural and ethnic prejudice.

I began the workshop by playing a YouTube clip of an episode of the FOX network game show *Are You Smarter Than a 5th Grader*, in which twenty-two-year-old country-pop singer-songwriter Kelly Pickler is asked to tackle the third-grade world geography question: "Budapest is the capital of what European country?"[2] As Pickler throws her hands up in the air in dismay and disbelief and Nathan, her fifth-grade fellow player, locks in with what will turn out to be the correct answer to the question, a jovial murmur ripples through the group of about fifteen workshop participants gathered around the long conference table. The murmur builds into a forceful chuckle as Pickler turns to Jeff Foxworthy, the show host, and announces with a languid Southern drawl, "This might be a stupid question ...," swells into hearty laughter at Foxworthy's retort, "I'm guessing it's probably gonna be," and bursts into full-blown guffawing at Pickler's actual question-*cum*-confession: "But, like, I thought Europe was a country!?" From here on to the end of the four-minute clip, the room is swept away on a rollercoaster ride of comic relief through the peaks and troughs of Pickler's display of blissful ignorance: "Budas ... Budapest ... I've never even heard of that! I know that they speak French there, don't they? Like, I wanna say, is France a country? I don't know what I'm doing!" And when, toward the end of the clip, upon being told by the show host that "the right answer is Hungary," Pickler blurts out, "Hungry? That's a country? Now, I've heard of Turkey!," the workshop participants are in stitches.

As I log off and close my laptop, the laughter subsides, giving way to what appears to be an awkward, tense silence—as if there were something shameful about giving free rein to one's limbic self at the expense of a blond twenty-two-year-old American pop star in this particular, culturally diverse setting.

In order to initiate a dialogue on what just happened, I ask the workshop participants what they think was so funny about the clip, and why they think they all laughed so hard. In the course of the group discussion that follows, three reasons are adduced by various workshop participants by way of explanation for their strong, visceral reactions to the clip.

The first reason, shared by German and US participants alike, is the sheer fact that *an adult person can be so ignorant and uneducated.* So unbelievable does Pickler's ignorance appear to be, in fact, that some of the workshop participants ask whether this is for real, or whether she is just acting dumb.

The second reason (also shared, as far as I can tell, by US and German participants of both sexes alike, even by the only two blond female participants) feeds directly into the first by bestowing a certain plausibility on what seemed incomprehensible from a squarely developmental viewpoint: *Pickler embodies and, thus, confirms the stereotype of the dumb blonde* (the Southern drawl doesn't help either, nor does her profession). In other words, because she happens to be a young, good-looking, blond woman, and a country-pop singer to boot (neither of which enjoys a high intellectual reputation), her ignorance—at first, a liability precisely because it did *not* meet certain, tacitly agreed-upon expectations regarding an average adult's horizon of knowledge—reveals itself as a kind of self-fulfilling prophecy: Being ignorant and dumb turns out to be precisely what one would expect of someone like Pickler.

The third reason, floated by a German participant, who is immediately seconded by several others, appears to create a palpable sense of discomfort and uneasiness around the table: *Pickler is living proof that Americans are dumb.* Again, an awkward, tense silence sets in, this time punctured by throat-clearing, body-posture-readjusting, and nervous leafing through my book (copies of which had been supplied to the attendees in advance of the workshop), which happens to begin with a set of critical reflections on the validity of two of the most prevalent prejudices among Germans against America and Americans, namely, that the latter are presumably dumb and uneducated.

As a group, the workshop participants have now reached a critical point in their conversation. All of a sudden, a sharp division into 'us' (Germans) and 'them' (Americans) has been introduced into what up to now seemed like a more or less cohesive, if by no means homogeneous, team of professionals gathered together for a specific, communally beneficial purpose. And not only that—clearly, 'they' have been assigned a lower rank in what appears to be (judging by the participants' shared approval of the first two reasons) the tacitly agreed-upon hierarchy of values among *all* participants, in which knowledge and intelligence would seem to occupy sufficiently elevated positions.

I cannot tell who among the workshop participants is more uncomfortable—the Americans or the

Germans who presumably think that Americans are 'dumb'. But, clearly, for both sides this must be a decisive moment, and a lot depends on how it will be resolved. The ones have divulged what they presumably *really* think about the others, while the latter now know what some of their fellow participants and coworkers *really* think about them. How to continue the conversation under these circumstances? How to move beyond this stalemate?

Suddenly, one of the German participants breaks the silence: "Of course, not all Americans are dumb!" Another immediately follows suit: "Yes, yes, one has to be careful ..." But, apparently, what's done is done, and these interventions don't seem to carry enough weight to undo the preceding gesture of blanket cultural denigration bespeaking deep-seated cultural resentment. Silence again takes over the conference room.

At this point, I suggest revisiting the clip and our reactions to it by way of defusing this somewhat volatile situation. One of the things that strikes me in particular, I point out to the workshop participants, is that, so far, nobody seems to have taken into account the fact that in the clip Pickler is in the minority. After all, the show host, fifth-grader Nathan, and—judging by their hearty laughter throughout Pickler's 'performance'—a sizable number of the members of the fairly large audience on the show as well, all seem to know the answer to the question that so flusters the blond singer. If anything, then, I suggest to my audience, the 'Pickler incident' would appear to be *living proof* that its protagonist is certainly *not* representative of Americans (or, for that matter, blond women) *in general.* "Yes, yes," one of the workshop participants impatiently cuts in, "why don't we ask who among those present knows the capital of Kyrgyzstan, or what country Bishkek is the capital of?"

This seems to be just the kind of punch line needed to pop the balloon of unease that has been hovering about the room for quite some time now and get the group out of the socio-cultural pickle it has gotten itself into.

"But, seriously," one of the German participants remarks after the laughter triggered by the Kyrgyzstan-Bishkek intervention has died down, "don't we *need* prejudice in order to make sense of the world around us, in order to orient ourselves? I mean, so often we cannot but rely on opinion, custom, stereotype, and prejudice if we want to find our bearings at all, can we?" "Well," I suggest, looking at the blond German woman who posed the question, "why don't we take one particular prejudice and see whether this is really the case? For instance, everybody knows that blondes are dumb, or that Germans are Nazis, right?"

~

Let me stop my account here and sum up what happened at the US Consulate that day: A bicultural group of highly educated and successful male and female professionals, gathered for the purpose of enhancing their understanding of the workings of prejudice with a view to applying the insights generated at the workshop productively in their respective professional and personal lives, succumbed to the seduction of prejudice *in spite of* being in the position to *know* first-hand that the prejudices activated by the 'Pickler incident' were not only unsustainable from a logical and broadly empirical standpoint (being 'dumb' is neither a function of hair color nor of nationality), but that they were also blatantly and palpably contradicted by the specific conditions of the workshop itself. For clearly, the Americans seated at the conference table as well as the two blond female participants ought to have been sufficient *living proof* for the implausibility of maintaining that Americans *in general* and blondes *in general* are 'dumb'.

At least one of the participants, moreover, appeared explicitly to subscribe to the popular theory according to which we *need* prejudice in order to be able to structure, make sense of, and navigate the world we live in—a theory that, as my somewhat provocative question suggested, would seem to cave in as soon as it is tested against reality.

What happened at the workshop is significant in three respects: (1) It throws into sharp relief that the common dissociation of prejudice and knowledge —the common view, that is, that prejudice is presumably predicated on *lack of knowledge* or *information*—is highly problematic and in need of rethinking. (2) It enjoins us to take a closer critical look at the popular view that we need prejudice in order to function. (3) It testifies to a sloppiness in conceptual thinking that contributes to the lumping together under the general head of 'prejudice' of all kinds of terms and senses that do *not* actually *mean* the phenomenon 'prejudice'—such as 'opinion', 'bias', 'custom', and 'stereotype'—and do, consequently, not have the same pragmatic impact as 'prejudice'.

~

This essay, as I suggested earlier, begins from the premise that prejudice is a purely nefarious phenomenon devoid of any positive value, an ideological toxin that eats away at the social fabric that sustains us. It thus goes against a long intellectual and cultural tradition extending all the way into the present that emphasizes the evolutionary, cognitive, and ethical value of prejudice, without which, as William Hazlitt famously observed, "I should not be able to find my way across the room; nor know how to conduct myself in any circumstances, nor what to feel in any relation of life."[3]

The exact opposite is maintained in these pages. Far from being a necessary aid for finding our bearings in this life and this world, prejudice is precisely what prevents us from seeing both for *what* they are and *as* they are. To the extent that, as philosopher

Ludwig Wittgenstein has argued, "the world is all that is the case," viewing the world through prejudice-colored glasses will necessarily distort "what is the case," whatever the case may be. This is not to suggest that a strictly *objective* apprehension of the world is even possible, but it is to remind ourselves that depending on how we look at the world, depending on the frameworks we use to interpret it, what we see will correspond more or less to "what is the case"; and in the case of prejudice, what we see will correspond rather less than more to "what is the case."[4]

The reason, I believe, that this positive view of prejudice has had such a long and successful career is twofold: On the one hand, the term 'prejudice' has been given senses that more properly belong to other terms—such as 'preconception', 'custom', 'received opinion', 'stereotype', and 'tradition'—and that capture aspects of our mental-social life without which we would, arguably, indeed be unable to function as social-historical beings dependent on the essentially generalizing thrust of language for thinking and communication.[5] On the other hand, this lumping together of a wide variety of senses under the general head of 'prejudice' has contributed to the dilution and occlusion of those semantic facets and nuances that can be said to be the distinguishing features of 'prejudice' *proper*—constituting its conceptual pith, which is, as I shall explain, *essentially negative*. Using 'prejudice' indiscriminately and interchangeably with such terms as 'preconception', 'custom', 'received opinion', 'bias', and 'stereotype' has not only led to the virtual stripping of 'prejudice' of its specific critical value as *the* term reserved for those opinions, preconceptions, and biases that imply and often lead to discrimination and violence, but, more importantly, it has also led to the *de facto* extenuation, belittlement, and trivialization of those attitudes, actions, and states of affairs that *only* the term 'prejudice' has been precise and powerful enough to capture and denote, and that appear in a much less severe and unflattering light if thought of euphemistically in such, overall 'benign', terms as 'tradition', 'custom', or 'opinion'.[6] One of the absurd consequences of this kind of confused and sloppy thinking about prejudice could be observed in my workshop: a blond woman arguing for the necessity of prejudice, including the one that blondes are presumably dumb.

What is needed, then, if we want to avoid these kinds of absurdities and the deleterious real-life consequences they entail, is as precise a definition of 'prejudice' as possible—a definition that will allow us clearly to demarcate 'prejudice' from other terms and concepts belonging to its semantic field, yet, as I shall explain, *essentially* distinct from it, and that will also help us to get a better sense of the relationship between prejudice and knowledge.

~

Before embarking on my conceptual journey, I should point out, by way of forestalling unnecessary terminological disputes, that in pursuing a precise definition of 'prejudice' I am not at all concerned with the *word* 'prejudice' as such but solely with the conceptual make-up of the discrete phenomenon that would seem to have consistently fallen within the fluid referential boundaries of 'prejudice' for many centuries and that no other term seems to have been capable of designating with equal precision and force. Which means that whatever word we may use to refer to the phenomenon in question, we will still be saddled with one and the same phenomenon in need of isolation, description, definition, and explication. For the sake of clarity, I have simply chosen to use the term that we commonly use to refer to and capture, among other things, what we *mean* when we use the term 'prejudice' in a strictly negative sense. Should you feel that another term better suits the phenomenon described in the following pages, I have no qualms with that, as long as we agree that we still mean the same phenomenon.

3

WHAT IS & WHAT IS NOT PREJUDICE

~

I have advanced the notion that the sense of 'prejudice' is essentially negative; and based on this notion, I have suggested that in real life, too, the impact of prejudice is a negative one. For this not to be a circular argument, what needs to be explained is in what way exactly 'prejudice' can be said to have an essentially negative sense. In other words, the distinguishing traits of 'prejudice', which separate it from all other terms it has too often been lumped together with to the great detriment of thinking and acting with clarity, need to be isolated and brought into sharp relief.

'Prejudice', it would appear, is one of those terms that wear their meaning on their sleeve. We all seem to know what it means, we all presumably recognize it when we see it. As its morphology suggests—'prejudice' derives from the Latin *praeiudicium* (*prae* = prior; *iudicium* = judgment, decision)—it is a judgment or decision about someone or something that *pre*cedes and is, consequently, devoid of something else. This 'something else', in turn, is typically taken to be 'knowledge', 'information', 'experience', 'evidence', or 'reason', judging by the following representative selection of commonly accepted definitions of 'prejudice', for instance, as:

- a "preconceived opinion that is not based on reason or experience" as well as "unjust behavior formed on such a basis" (*Oxford English Dictionary*)

- a "preconceived judgment or opinion," an "adverse opinion or leaning formed without just grounds or before sufficient knowledge," an "instance of such judgment or opinion," as well as an "irrational attitude of hostility directed against an individual, a group, a race, or their supposed characteristics" (*Merriam-Webster's Collegiate Dictionary*)

- an "unfavorable opinion or feeling formed beforehand or without knowledge, thought or reason," a "preconceived opinion or feeling, either favorable or unfavorable," any "unreasonable feelings, opinions, or attitudes, esp. of a hostile nature, regarding a racial, religious, or national group," as well as "such attitudes considered collectively" (*Dictionary.com*)

- "negative beliefs, attitudes, or feelings about a person's entire character based on only one characteristic" and often on "faulty information" (*Virtual Psychology Classroom*)

- "a baseless and usually negative attitude toward members of a group" (*Dictionary of Psychological Terms*)

- "prejudgment: making a decision before becoming aware of the relevant facts" (*Wikipedia.org*)
- "all opinions held without sufficient information or sufficient practical experience" (French *Wikipédia.org*).

Similar definitions can be found, for instance, in the French *Dictionnaire des Sciences Philosophiques (Dictionary of the Philosophical Sciences)*, the German *Wörterbuch der philosophischen Grundbegriffe (Dictionary of Basic Philosophical Terms)*, and elsewhere.

For the sake of clarity and concision, I would like to offer the following, logically sufficient, composite definition of the received meaning of 'prejudice' as a point of departure for the subsequent discussion:

> A prejudice is a favorable or unfavorable attitude toward, opinion on, or judgment about someone or something (an individual or a group) predicated on lack of or insufficient knowledge, information, evidence, experience, or reason to support or justify such an attitude, opinion, or judgment.

It goes without saying that the condition of *just ground* or *sufficient reason* more or less explicitly at work in all of the above definitions relies on a broad, 'objective', commonsense understanding of what constitutes sufficient "knowledge, information, evidence, experience, or reason." (I should note at this point that I am not specifically concerned here with the legal sense of 'prejudice' understood, according to *Merriam-Webster's Collegiate Dictionary*, as "injury or damage resulting from some judgment or action of another in disregard of one's rights," or "detriment to one's legal rights or claims," and known to us from the legal phrase "without prejudice." As my discussion will show, however, the term's legal sense dovetails with its overall negative thrust.[1])

So far, so good—at least, as far as definitions go. But does the definition of the received meaning of 'prejudice' actually correspond to its *real-life sense*, to our *real-life* understanding and use of 'prejudice'? In other words, do we actually think of all those situations that are presumably captured by the composite definition in terms of 'prejudice'?

Let us consider the following examples:

(1) You decide to get married on the spur of the moment to a person whom you only recently met, whom you have fallen in love with 'head over heels', and whom you judge—without, 'objectively' speaking, having sufficient reasonable grounds to support your judgment and the life-altering decision it entails—to be the most appropriate partner for you to go through life with.

(2) During the Third Reich, many Germans believed that Jews were dirty, conniving, conspiratorial, and dangerous.

(3) A person certified to be suffering from paranoid delusions believes that all contemporary Germans are Nazis.

(4) Apparently, a sizable number of Muslims in the Middle East who have never been to the US and have hardly had *sufficient* first-hand exposure to Americans have negative views about the US and its citizens. Similarly, many Americans who have never been to Europe believe that the French are arrogant and that Germans are obsessed with order.

Which of these instances, would you say, warrants being conceived of in terms of 'prejudice'? Who among the persons in these examples, would you say, thinks or acts 'with prejudice'?

Let us take example (1). I seriously doubt that any of your friends who scoff at your decision to get married on the spur of the moment to a person you hardly know, and who try to dissuade you from such a step would even remotely think of your lover's blindness in terms of 'prejudice', let alone call you 'prejudiced in favor' of your lover. 'Prejudice' simply doesn't seem to apply here. They might call you or your decision 'dumb', 'stupid', 'rash', 'foolhardy', 'hysterical', 'deluded', 'irrational', but not, I venture to say, 'prejudiced'. Yet, your judgment and decision fall squarely within the composite definition of the received meaning of 'prejudice', insofar as, 'objectively' speaking, both would appear to rely on "insufficient knowledge, information, experience, or reason."

Let us now look at example (2). In this instance, it is fair to say that nobody in his right mind would call Nazi attitudes and behavior toward Jews anything but 'prejudiced'. In fact, this is precisely the kind of situation to which the notion of 'prejudice' emphatically applies—a model instance of prejudice.

Yet, if we consider this example in light of the composite definition of the received meaning of 'prejudice', we cannot fail to observe that it doesn't fit it as neatly as one would expect a model to match its design. For in view of Germans' and Jews' centuries-long shared history and symbiotic coexistence, which reached an historical peak precisely in the first half of the twentieth century, it would be implausible (if not outright preposterous) to suggest—as historians, eyewitnesses to the Holocaust (both Germans and Jews), and, in particular, those ethnic Germans who resisted the Nazis domestically and from abroad have taught us—that, generally speaking, ethnic Germans in the 1930s hadn't had sufficient interaction with their Jewish fellow Germans (most of whom were secular and blended right in with the rest of the country) to know as much about them as about anybody among their fellow Germans, and that, consequently, their attitudes and behavior toward Jews were "predicated on lack of or insufficient knowledge, information, evidence, [and] experience." Barring the latter, however, the treatment of Jews in the Third Reich can only be called 'prejudiced', according to the composite definition of the received meaning of 'prejudice', insofar as it can be said to have, at the very least, been predicated on "lack of or insufficient reason to support or justify" such treatment as well as the attitudes, opinions, and judgments it was motivated by.

What does this mean exactly? Given that Third-Reich Germans have been established to have had sufficient "knowledge, information, evidence, [and] experience" with regard to their Jewish fellow Germans, "lack of or insufficient reason" in this context must *not* be read, as the composite definition would seem to suggest, as merely expanding on and further specifying "insufficient knowledge, information, evidence, [and] experience," but, rather, as bespeaking the exact opposite, namely: possession of *sufficient* "knowledge, information, evidence, [and] experience" *not* to support or justify those attitudes, opinions, and judgments that led to the Holocaust. In other words, Germans during the Third Reich who subscribed to Nazi views on Jews can be said to have had insufficient reason to do so *not* because they lacked enough information and evidence as to what was going on, but, on the contrary, because they did have *sufficient* information and evidence at the very least strongly to suspect that Nazi doctrine *did not* jibe with reality.

And while Nazi-Germany's anti-Semitism could be (and, indeed, has been) called 'irrational' in an imprecise, colloquial sense, this 'irrationality' must not in any way be identified with the composite definition's "lack of or insufficient reason," which doesn't signify 'madness' or 'delusion' so much as 'having no grounds or reasonable justification' (as in 'I have no reason to believe that').

Which brings us to example (3). We would hardly use the term 'prejudice' to describe a paranoiac's belief that all contemporary Germans are Nazis because the very notion of 'prejudice', it would seem, presupposes mental competence, a sufficiently sound or rational state of mind on the part of the person considered holding prejudice—a state of mind, that is, in which the person can be held (fully) accountable for his or her thoughts and actions. If anything, the paranoiac's assessment of contemporary Germans' ideological views would have to be called 'irrational' or 'delusional'.

The *sound mind* condition of prejudice, in turn, implies that 'prejudice' presupposes a certain level of mental development and intellectual maturity. Thus, we would most likely not call a three-and-a-half-year-old who says that he doesn't like 'black people' 'prejudiced'—though we would probably suspect that he is being raised in a deeply prejudiced environment.

Example (4), finally, is somewhat more complicated. On the one hand, we would probably use the term 'prejudice'—in a lax and general manner—in reference to anti-American sentiment among Muslims in the Middle East who haven't had sufficient first-hand experience with the US and Americans, as well as Americans who hold forth against France and Germany without having been sufficiently exposed to their cultures and relying mostly on hearsay and second-hand opinion. In fact, it is precisely this kind of attitude that is captured by the composite definition's "lack of or insufficient knowledge, information, evidence, experience, or reason."

On the other hand, we would have to ask: Is, then, any opinion, preconception, or bias—whether acquired through hearsay or association with others (who may or may not be truly prejudiced)—necessarily prejudice? This can hardly be the case, as then everything we learn and know about the world that we haven't seen with our own eyes and verified for ourselves and cannot but accept as true on faith, based on our trust in those who provide the information in question, would have to count as prejudice. This, in turn, would not only make the term 'prejudice' virtually inoperable as a critical concept on account of excessive semantic breadth, but it would also, dubiously, imply (given that learning from others is an essential aspect of human development) that holding prejudice is an anthropological necessity.[2]

Thus, upon further reflection, we ought probably not to use the term 'prejudice' in reference to the situations described in the final example but, rather, 'preconception', 'opinion', or 'bias', for instance.

In view of these considerations, it has become clear that the received meaning of 'prejudice' doesn't seem to be sufficiently adequate for capturing the complexities of the term's actual use and ought, consequently, to be adjusted. Taking my cue from the one example that we would most likely unanimously agree upon thinking of in terms of 'prejudice'—anti-Semitism during the Third Reich—I suggest modifying the initial composite definition—

> a prejudice is a favorable or unfavorable attitude toward, opinion on, or judgment about someone or something (an individual or a group) predicated on lack of or insufficient knowledge, information, evidence, experience, or reason to support or justify such an attitude, opinion, or judgment

—as follows:

> A prejudice is a favorable or unfavorable attitude toward, opinion on, or judgment about someone or something (an individual or a group) **held by a person of sound mind in spite of sufficient** knowledge, information, evidence, experience, or reason **not** to support or justify such an attitude, opinion, or judgment.

This revised definition to the effect that what makes our biases, opinions, and preconceptions prejudice is the fact that we continue maintaining them even in the face of controverting evidence (for instance, by *rationalizing* them) is vividly borne out by the bemusing prejudicial behavior on the part of some of the participants in my workshop at the US Consulate General in Düsseldorf, who were in the position to *know* that their cultural and ethnic prejudices were empirically unsustainable.

If, however, we allow any of our given biases, opinions, or preconceptions to be 'corrected' by reality (should we suspect them to be untenable, or should we determine them to be wrong), then we do not succumb to the seduction of prejudice.[3]

~

But can this really be the whole story? Does this mean that any attitude toward, opinion on, or judgment about someone or something that we know to be contradicted by facts or other kinds of evidence is *necessarily* prejudice? Again, let us look at several examples that will help us clarify this issue:

(1) A woman happens to think that her husband is the most brilliant, attractive, and desirable man in the world even though, 'objectively' speaking—that is, based on reigning standards of intelligence testing, beauty, and sexuality—this would not seem to be the case.

(2) The manager of a company interviews two highly qualified job applicants. Although he determines that the female applicant is better qualified for

the job, he goes for the male applicant because he believes, unreasonably, that he will do a better job than his female competitor.

(3) Although a father suspects that others may be better suited and qualified than his son to succeed him as head of the family business, he decides to ask his son to take over—without even looking for a successor outside the family—in the hope that his son will learn the ropes on the job.

Which of these three instances would you be inclined to think of in terms of 'prejudice'?

As far as example (1) is concerned, it is probably safe to say that nobody would call one spouse's favorable attitude toward the other 'prejudice' even if, 'objectively' speaking, this attitude may not be justified; 'blinded by love', perhaps, or 'irrational', 'deluded', 'unrealistic', 'incomprehensible', or simply 'that's what love and marriage are all about'—but not 'prejudice'.

The company manager's hiring decision in example (2), on the other hand, would probably be agreed upon as qualifying as a prime instance of prejudice under the revised definition.

Example (3), finally, would seem to fit the revised definition of 'prejudice' as well; yet, I think, we would not call the father's decision to ask his son to take over the family business 'prejudicial'.

What is it that makes example (2) a prime instance of prejudice, while examples (1) and (3) would not be considered such? It is, I suggest, the force of a particular *intent*, which may be implicit or explicit, and what this intent entails that makes all the difference.

What do I mean by this? What makes example (2) a prime instance of prejudice is the fact that the manager's hiring decision is predicated on the implicit derogation of and detraction from another candidate.

Let me explain: Unlike one spouse's boundless admiration for the other in example (1), or a father's decision to ask his son to succeed him as head of the family business in example (3)—both of which are predicated on favorable attitudes toward and judgments about persons that do not simultaneously involve and are not functionally dependent on negative judgments about other persons—the manager's decision in example (2) to favor one candidate over the other is predicated precisely on the concomitant derogation of and detraction from the latter. In other words, one spouse's admiration for the other in example (1) and a father's decision to ask his son to succeed him in example (3) do not carry an *implicit or explicit intent to diminish the value of a third party* (be it another's spousal virtues or professional expertise, respectively), whereas the manager's hiring decision in example (2) does.

What makes the manager's action prejudicial is the fact that his favorable attitude or bias toward his applicant of choice concomitantly implies the other applicant's devaluation. (And even if the manager ostensibly succeeded in *rationalizing* his hiring decision in the most philanthropic terms—for instance, by convincing himself that he is actually doing the female applicant a favor by not hiring her for what will, no doubt, be a terribly taxing job—such rationalizing could not fail to betray an underlying condonation of the tacit devaluation of the applicant not hired, given that the very notion of 'rationalizing' implies a more or less suppressed awareness on the rationalizer's part that his decisions and actions might be predicated on "lack of or insufficient reason"—otherwise there would be no need to rationalize.)

In light of these considerations, the definition of 'prejudice' needs yet again to be amended to capture this added complexity of *comparative valuation* (which is more or less overtly at work in both favorable and unfavorable prejudice), and *implicit or explicit derogatory intent regarding a third party*, more generally (which, as we shall see, plays out slightly differently in favorable and unfavorable prejudice, respectively).[4] Thus, the new revised definition reads:

> A prejudice is a favorable or unfavorable attitude toward, opinion on, or judgment about someone or something (an individual or a group) held by a person of sound mind in spite of sufficient knowledge, information, evidence, experience, or reason not to support or justify such an attitude, opinion, or judg-

ment, **and carrying an implicit or explicit intent to denigrate, derogate, or detract from someone or something else**.

This new addition to the definition of 'prejudice' is of crucial importance. It casts the very notion of the so-called 'favorable prejudice' in not as favorable a light as the name suggests and goes a long way in explaining my claim that the sense of 'prejudice' is, at bottom, a negative one and that, consequently, in real life, too, the impact of prejudice is a negative one.

What do I mean? Simply this: A prejudice in favor of someone or something implies the devaluation of someone or something else. Thus, if we revisit the example of the manager who hires the male and not the female applicant, although he has determined *her* to be better qualified for the job than *him*, in the light of the manager's favorable prejudice toward the male applicant, we cannot fail to be thrown back on the manager's concomitant unfavorable prejudice against the female applicant.

This binary logic applies to all forms of favorable (and unfavorable) prejudice, insofar as prejudice as such has been said to hinge on comparative valuation. On closer inspection, the very term 'favorable prejudice' reveals itself as simply meaning 'prejudice' viewed through the lens of the one 'benefiting' from it; analogously, 'unfavorable prejudice' simply means 'prejudice' viewed from the perspective of the one being detracted from. When prejudice is at work, someone always suffers in one way or another.

At this point, we can begin demarcating 'prejudice' from other terms that belong to its semantic field, such as 'belief', 'opinion', 'preconception', 'conviction', 'cliché', 'attitude', 'preference', 'viewpoint', 'bias', and 'stereotype'. For now, let me note by way of a first step that what distinguishes 'prejudice' proper from these terms (and others that could be added) is that only 'prejudice' can be said to be predicated on the dual condition of an awareness of *sufficient evidence to the contrary* and an *implicit or explicit derogatory intent regarding a third party*. In other words, while terms such as 'belief', 'opinion', 'preconception', 'conviction', 'cliché', 'attitude', 'preference', 'viewpoint', 'bias', and 'stereotype' may meet one of the two conditions or both, they do not have to meet either condition in order to fulfill their semantic and pragmatic purpose. For our hands-on thinking about prejudice this means, for instance, that—to go back to the intervention of the participant in my workshop at the US Consulate General in Düsseldorf who appeared to subscribe to the theory that we *need* opinion, custom, stereotype, and prejudice in order to find our bearings in this world—while we might indeed not be able to live and function in society and the world at large without custom, tradition, opinion, preconception, and stereotype, this doesn't entail that we also *need* prejudice.

~

Let us return to the second revised definition of 'prejudice'—

> a prejudice is a favorable or unfavorable attitude toward, opinion on, or judgment about someone or something (an individual or a group) held by a person of sound mind in spite of sufficient knowledge, information, evidence, experience, or reason not to support or justify such an attitude, opinion, or judgment, **and carrying an implicit or explicit intent to denigrate, derogate, or detract from someone or something else**

—and further reflect on its final component: *implicit or explicit derogatory intent regarding a third party*. What this effectively means is that prejudice is never directed at only one entity but always refers to more than one object, that it has, as I explain in the next chapter, by definition, a *string* of referents. It is at this point that we glimpse yet another level of the fundamental make-up of the concept of 'prejudice'—the level of what I call the *strings of prejudice.*

4

THE STRING THEORY OF PREJUDICE

~

What does it mean to say that by definition prejudice is directed at a *string of referents*?

It means that all judgments, attitudes, beliefs, and opinions that only refer to a single object—whether positively or negatively—simply do not make the cut for 'prejudice'. For instance, saying, "This movie is dumb" or "I love France," is simply articulating an opinion, attitude, belief, conviction, or state of heart, and functions along the same lines as some of the above examples (falling in love, spousal affection, filial succession in the family business). However, saying, "This movie is dumb, like most Hollywood movies," or "I love France, it is simply so civilized compared to the other European countries," would be a first step in the direction of prejudice.

The *plural reference* or *string of referents* condition is predicated on the following recognition: Prejudice, by its very nature, relies on abstraction and generalization and engages its target not as a singularity, as this unique, incomparable, irreplaceable being or object, but, rather, as an *instance* or *occurrence* standing in for an entire *class* or *type* of objects; consequently, prejudice cannot but refer to the entire class or type instanced by the object it happens to be concretely directed at. (In the case of unfavorable prejudice in particular, this means that the *implicit or explicit intent to denigrate, derogate, or detract from someone or something else* runs parallel to its overall generalizing thrust. Whereas in the case of favorable prejudice the derogated third party contrasts with the concrete object of prejudice, functioning as an axiological foil against which the latter is favorably assessed, in the case of outright unfavorable prejudice the derogated third party is viewed precisely as *not* axiologically distinct from, as *belonging to the same class or type as* the concrete object of prejudice.)

Thus, to go back to the example of the manager who hires the male rather than the female job applicant, although the latter is better qualified, on the basis of his conviction that the former will simply do a better job on account of being male: What makes this a prime instance of prejudice is not only that the manager doesn't happen to like *this* one person, who happens to be a woman, in her capacity as a professional but that he doesn't favor her, insofar as she is an instance of an entire class of persons (women), all members of which are necessarily referenced and negatively affected by his judgment; concomitantly, the manager doesn't simply happen to like *this* one person, who happens to be a man, in his capacity as a professional—rather, he favors him *qua* instance of an entire class of persons (men), all members of which are automatically favorably affected by his judgment. Thus, the comparative valuation that is ostensibly limited to the male and female applicants is, in fact, a comparative valuation between two classes or types of persons: men and women.

Similarly, if we look at the example of loving France because "it is simply so civilized compared to the other European countries," we cannot but detect signs of prejudice, insofar as in this statement France is no longer viewed simply as 'France' (as in the example "I love France")—as a singular place with which I may happen to associate childhood, first love, happy school days, reading Proust, etc.—but as representative of the class of people and things constituting and defined in terms of 'civilization', which is in turn used as an axiological metric.

In practical terms, this means, for instance, that you cannot dislike just one Jew or Muslim or Christian or American or German, insofar as you consider any given Jew, Muslim, Christian, American, or German in terms of his being Jewish, Muslim, Christian, American, or German, all of which necessarily imply being perceived as an instance or occurrence of a class or type, respectively; conversely, you cannot love one Jew, Muslim, Christian, American, or German and be anti-Semitic, anti-Muslim, anti-Christian, anti-American, or anti-German at the same time—at least, insofar as we conceive of 'love' (as we commonly do) as not predicated on the obfuscation or suppression of core aspects of any given beloved's identity and insofar as we view ethnicity, religious affiliation, and national identity (as we commonly do) as constitutive of personal identity—because in being anti-Semitic, anti-Muslim, anti-Christian, anti-American, or anti-German you automatically position yourself negatively *vis-à-vis* your Jewish, Muslim, Christian, American, or German 'beloved'.[1] Similarly, you cannot love one lawyer and hate lawyers at the same time, insofar as being a lawyer can be said to form part of your beloved's identity.

In light of these considerations, the definition of 'prejudice' must yet again be modified to incorporate the *string of referents* condition—the fact that in order to pass as 'prejudice' an opinion, attitude, or judgment has to meet not only the conditions already laid out but also treat its object as a mere instance or occurrence of a class or type, that is, essentially refer to a plurality. Thus, the new revised definition reads:

> A prejudice is a favorable or unfavorable attitude toward, opinion on, or judgment about someone or something **considered as a mere instance or occurrence of a class or type—and thus, by definition, directed at a string of referents**—held by a person of sound mind in spite of sufficient knowledge, information, evidence, experience, or reason not to support or justify such an attitude, opinion, or judgment, and carrying an implicit or explicit

intent to denigrate, derogate, or detract from someone or something else.

~

Have we now reached a comprehensive understanding of 'prejudice'? Let us look at several examples, including two previous cases, that we would agree upon viewing as instances of prejudice and put the new revised definition to the test:

(1) A person considered of sound mind believes that pigeons are carriers of deadly disease and ought to be exterminated.

(2) The same person also believes that left-handed children are intellectually less well endowed than right-handed children and ought not to be admitted into AP programs in schools.

(3) During the Third Reich, many Germans believed that Jews were dirty, conniving, conspiratorial, and dangerous, that they ought to be kept out of German schools and work places, and deserved to be exterminated.

(4) The manager of a company interviews two highly qualified job applicants. Although he determines that the female applicant is better qualified for the job, he chooses to offer the position to the male applicant because he believes, unreasonably, that the latter will do a better job than the former.

It is safe to say that we would not conceive of the situation depicted in example (1) in terms of 'prejudice'. Most likely, we would call a person's opinion that pigeons ought to be exterminated for the reason provided 'misguided', 'misinformed', 'deluded', 'irrational', or 'crazy' (in the colloquial sense) but not an instance of prejudice, in spite of the fact that it meets the conditions laid out in the new revised definition, including the most recently added *string of referents* condition (pigeons *in general*).

The same applies, it seems to me, to example (2), even though the fact that in this instance the person's opinion pertains to a particular group of persons would seem to suggest that we are now more obviously entering the territory of prejudice. Here, too, I venture to say, we would call the belief that left-handed students ought to be kept out of AP programs for the reason provided 'misguided', 'misinformed', 'deluded', 'irrational', or 'crazy' (in the colloquial sense) and not an instance of prejudice; again, in spite of the fact that it satisfies the conditions laid out in the new revised definition, including the *string of referents* condition (left-handed children *in general*).

As far as examples (3) and (4) are concerned, it is safe to say that the treatment of Jews during the Third Reich as well as the manager's gender-biased hiring decision are aptly captured by the term 'prejudice'. Given that all four cases meet all of the conditions laid out in the new revised definition of 'prejudice', why are not all four instances of prejudice? What is it that distinguishes examples (1) and (2) from examples (3) and (4)? For whatever it is that is structurally missing in the first two situations and that is present in the latter two must be a necessary component of 'prejudice'.

What distinguishes these two sets of examples is the fact that in the first two only one person holds certain opinions about pigeons and left-handed children, whereas in the second set a plurality of persons have certain attitudes towards Jews and women, respectively. Example (4) is especially illuminating: On the surface, it would seem to parallel the pigeon-hater's and anti-left-handed-children advocate's situations, as here, in (4), too, only one person is judging and acting 'with prejudice'. However, the fact that the manager is alone and acts individually should not make us forget the concomitant fact that those beliefs and attitudes of his that warrant our unqualified assessment of his action as prejudicial have been shared by many others. If he were alone in believing that a woman cannot do the job as well as a man although she is better qualified, he, too, like the pigeon hater and anti-left-handed-children advocate, would most likely have to be considered not 'prejudiced' but 'misguided', 'irrational', 'deluded', or 'crazy'.

We have reached another insight: Not only is it necessary for an opinion, attitude, or judgment to be considered prejudice to meet all the conditions mentioned, but it is also requisite that it have more than one proponent, that it have a *string of proponents*. The definition of 'prejudice' needs to be amended yet again, this time, to incorporate the *string of proponents* condition. Thus, the new revised definition reads:

> A prejudice is a favorable or unfavorable attitude toward, opinion on, or judgment about someone or something considered as a mere instance or occurrence of a class or type—and thus, by definition, directed at a string of referents—**held by a string of proponents** of sound mind in spite of sufficient knowledge, information, evidence, experience, or reason not to support or justify such an attitude, opinion, or judgment, and carrying an implicit or explicit intent to denigrate, derogate, or detract from someone or something else.

~

To complete the definition, it seems to me, one more string needs to be accounted for as part of prejudice's genetic make-up. Let us again consider several examples, including some of the previous cases, beginning with the prejudices discussed in my book *17 Prejudices That We Germans Hold Against America and Americans and That Can't Quite Be True.*

(1) Among Germans, you will frequently encounter the following assertions: Americans are dumb, uneducated, and uncultured; they don't speak any other languages and have no taste; they are loud, fat, and eat only fast food; Coca-Cola and McDonald's are to blame for all evils; Hollywood is 'crap'; America wants to rule the world.[2]

(2) Among Americans, conversely, you will frequently encounter the following views about Germans: They are obsessed with order and organizing; they are obsessively punctual, serious, rule-driven, meticulous, and, somehow, still Nazis.

(3) During the Third Reich, many Germans believed that Jews were dirty, conniving, conspiratorial, and dangerous.

(4) The manager of a company interviews two highly qualified job applicants. Although he determines that the female applicant is better qualified for the job, he goes for the male applicant because he believes that women are not as intelligent, enduring, and 'tough' as men; that they are emotional, illogical, and unreliable; and that as soon as the female applicant is hired she will want to have children and will request maternity leave.

What all of these examples show (and, obviously, many more could be added) is that those who hold any given prejudice do not hold only *one* prejudice against a *string of referents* but more than one. Prejudice never comes alone but always with a *string* of other prejudices in tow that together form a network or cluster of prejudices around any given referent. Moreover, any given *string of prejudices* held by a *string of proponents* against a *string of referents* follows a certain pattern or logic; in other words, a *string of prejudices* is not simply a random congeries of attitudes and beliefs about someone or something but a more or less coherent catalogue of features that we would classify as going together based on certain semantic criteria.

Let us take example (1) and trace the logic underlying this *string of prejudices.* Clearly, it is plausible that if you believe someone to be 'dumb' that you might also assert that he is 'uneducated', both of which, in turn, are easily associated with lack of 'culture' in general; of course, those who have been determined to be 'uncultured', the argument goes, cannot possibly speak foreign languages, have taste, or know how to 'behave'; moreover, the argument continues, since physical aesthetics and culinary sophistication form part of what it means to be 'cultured', 'uncultured' folk will be physically unappealing (of which being fat is presumably an extreme form) and eat 'crap' (which makes them fat); those, in turn, the argument maintains, responsible for producing and proliferating 'crap' and 'non-culture' (including 'material crap' such as fast food, epitomized by Coca-Cola and McDonald's, and 'intellectual crap', epitomized by 'Hollywood') must be blamed; finally, the argument concludes, it's not enough that *they* eat 'crap', must they also spread *their* 'crap' around the world and impose *their* lack of 'culture' and *their* way of life on *us*?

A similar logic of concatenation underlies the other examples. Suffice it to revisit case (2). Thus, if you believe that somebody is obsessed with order and organizing, it is not implausible also to conceive of him as being obsessively serious, punctual, and meticulous ("Just think of the German railroad system and how the trains are always on time in Germany—not like Italy!"). From here, it is only a small step to making the leap back to the Nazis (the "most organized, meticulous, rule-driven, and order-obsessed of all")—and *their* railroad system ...[3]

In light of these considerations, the definition of 'prejudice' must yet again be amended to include reference to this newly discovered component of its DNA. The final, complete definition reads:

> A prejudice is a favorable or unfavorable attitude toward, opinion on, or judgment about someone or something considered as a mere instance or occurrence of a class or type—and thus, by definition, directed at a string of referents—held by a string of proponents of sound mind in spite of sufficient knowledge, information, evidence, experience, or reason not to support or justify such an attitude, opinion, or judgment, carrying an implicit or explicit intent to denigrate, derogate, or detract from someone or something else, and **coming with a string of prejudices in tow**.

Thus, for an opinion, attitude, or judgment to be considered prejudice, the following six conditions have to be met: (1) the *sound mind* condition; (2) the *sufficient evidence to the contrary* condition; (3) the *implicit or explicit derogatory intent regarding a third party* condition; (4) the *string of referents* condition; (5) the *string of proponents* condition; (6) the *string of prejudices* condition. This, I suggest, is the basic molecular structure, the DNA of prejudice. And only if all of these conditions are met does it make sense to speak of 'prejudice'—if, that is, we don't want to dilute the concept of 'prejudice' *and*, concomitantly, taint or contaminate other, more innocuous concepts, with its disease.

5

FIRST PRACTICAL CONSEQUENCES

~

Equipped with this clear grasp of what 'prejudice' means and how it works conceptually, we can begin paying closer attention to the ways in which it and its conceptual siblings and cousins manifest themselves in real life, without being continuously uncertain as to whether we are dealing with prejudice in any given situation or not.

The practical importance of understanding the difference between 'prejudice' and its conceptual relatives cannot be overestimated as our responses to and interaction with others will be profoundly informed by our intentional assessment of what they think or say—of how and why they think what they think and say what they say and with what intentions or goals. In other words, how we respond to and engage with others will be very much determined by whether we think that they are merely voicing an opinion, belief, conviction, preconception, attitude, preference, bias, perspective, or viewpoint; whether they are merely stating or repeating a cliché, commonplace, or stereotype; or whether they are truly prejudiced in the strong sense of our definition.

Our first attempt to demarcate 'prejudice' from its conceptual relatives yielded the minimal logical insight that only 'prejudice' satisfies the dual condition of an awareness of *sufficient evidence to the contrary* and an *implicit or explicit derogatory intent regarding a third party*, while 'opinion', 'belief', 'conviction', 'preconception', 'attitude', 'preference', 'bias', 'perspective', 'viewpoint', 'cliché', 'commonplace', or 'stereotype' *may* satisfy one of the two conditions or both but *do not have to* satisfy either in order to fulfill their semantic and social-pragmatic purpose.

This demarcation, however, did not yet allow us to determine with *reasonable certainty* whether in any given situation we are dealing with prejudice or simply a negative or derogatory opinion, belief, or attitude on the part of someone who, we may suspect, *knows* the opinion, attitude, or belief to be unjustified or false. Thus, even if someone's speech or behavior satisfies both conditions (*sufficient evidence to the contrary* and *implicit or explicit derogatory intent regarding a third party*), under our preliminary demarcation we will only be able to state with reasonable certainty that it *could* or *might* bespeak prejudice. Now, however, we realize that the latter is only the case if *all* six conditions of prejudice are met.

The comprehensive definition of 'prejudice' easily lends itself to real-life application and will help us to detect prejudice with reasonable certainty when we see it and to know with reasonable certainty what is not prejudice even though it may sound and look like it. For *what is not prejudice may satisfy some but does not satisfy all six conditions of prejudice.*

What does this mean in practical terms? It means, for instance, that if, in any given situation, we determine that a person voices a prejudice and not merely an opinion, bias, attitude, or conviction with regard to someone or something that we happen to disagree with, we will understand that trying to persuade and convince that person that he is factually wrong, that things are not the way he thinks they are would be redundant and most likely lead nowhere because our determination that we are confronted with prejudice already implies the recognition that the one holding the prejudice in question *knows* that it is not 'true', that it is factually untenable. (As we all probably know, so many discussions and arguments revolving around prejudicial behavior get bogged down in exasperating attempts to teach the one holding prejudice something he already knows: that he cannot be factually correct.) This, in turn, means that we will not waste time and energy on 'preaching to the converted' but will, from the get-go, think of more inventive strategies for parrying the prejudice we happen to be confronted with—such as, for instance, the one intuitively deployed by one of the participants in my workshop at the US Consulate General in Düsseldorf, who, in response to another participant's assertion that "Americans are dumb" in view of Kelly Pickler's ignorance in world geography, suggested, "Why don't we ask who among those present knows the capital of Kyrgyzstan, or what country Bishkek is the capital of?," instead of attempting to reason with and enlighten his fellow workshop participants.

Alternatively, if, in any given situation, we determine that we are *not* confronted with prejudice but with a belief, attitude, or opinion that we believe to be or happen to know to be false, we will know, for instance, that trying to explain to our interlocutor that he might be factually mistaken may be a sensible path to take in the conversation, as it could be that he simply doesn't *know* that his belief or opinion is factually implausible or false and might be amenable to changing his views upon being shown controverting evidence. This is not to say, however, that explaining to someone who happens to be articulating a false belief or opinion that he is mistaken or wrong is the way to go in any given situation, as the person in question might not be amenable to being told, by you or anybody else, at this particular moment, that he is wrong.

Thus, what we *de facto* decide to do in any given situation depends on a number of factors exceeding our conceptual grasp of the workings of prejudice—including, among other things, the situational context and an intuitive assessment of our interlocutor's state of mind. However, in order to be able to engage in the most appropriate and productive course of action, being able to determine what it is we are dealing with—prejudice or something else— cannot but be immensely helpful.

The following example illustrates this point: Several years ago, I had relatives from Russia staying with me in Manhattan. One day, they decided to visit another set of relatives who lived in the Bronx. As they were preparing for their day trip, they told me that they were afraid to take the subway to 242nd Street because the first time they had taken the One-Train from Penn Station uptown there had been many blacks on the subway and they had felt very uncomfortable. My response was to wax judgmental about the racial prejudice still rampant in my country of origin with the end result of a dispute and my relatives from the Bronx having to come down to Manhattan and pick up my house guests by car.

Had I had the presence of mind, however, not to jump to conclusions and judge my visitors, *and* had I known about prejudice what I know about it now, I might have noticed, for instance, that in expressing their *apprehension* they were not really articulating prejudice (under the comprehensive definition), for given that this was their first time in the US and given that they had not been exposed to African-Americans before, their attitude did not satisfy the *sufficient evidence to the contrary* condition; based on this realization, in turn, I might not have, unthinkingly, interpreted their comment as automatically bespeaking prejudice and responded in a manner more commensurate with the fact that whatever we may want to call their comment and however we may want classify it—as 'stereotype', 'preconception', or 'bias', for instance—it did not satisfy all six conditions of prejudice. (If anything, my relatives' attitude and behavior can be said to have fit the initial composite definition of the received meaning of 'prejudice', which has been shown to fall short of capturing the complexity of the *actual* phenomenon of prejudice).

What we *do* once we have determined whether what we are confronted with is prejudice or not is not our immediate concern at this juncture, but it is clear that we are in a much better position to do whatever we determine the right thing to do in any given situation if we know *what* we are dealing with, prejudice or something else. And it makes a big difference whether we consider something an opinion we may want to agree or disagree with, a conviction we may want to respect or disregard, a belief we may want to attempt to alter or acquiesce to, a stereotype we may simply want to brush aside or concur with, or a veritable prejudice that needs to be countered.

6

THE TENACITY OF PREJUDICE

~

We have now reached the point at which a reasonable explanation can be advanced as to why prejudice might be so persistent and tenacious, on the basis of its very conceptual structure and prior to all psychological, socio-cultural, and political-historical considerations.

Let us recall the six conditions of prejudice: (1) the *sound mind* condition; (2) the *sufficient evidence to the contrary* condition; (3) the *implicit or explicit derogatory intent regarding a third party* condition; (4) the *string of referents* condition; (5) the *string of proponents* condition; (6) the *string of prejudices* condition. While all six comprehensively capture the molecular structure of prejudice, it is, as we shall see, the reticulation of the last three in particular that firmly holds the entire structure in place, rooting it firmly in the soil of personality, culture, and history.

Let me elaborate this by resorting to a metaphor. Think of a tree in a forest, with foliage, branches, trunk, and roots that are intertwined with the roots of the trees immediately surrounding it, and so on with all the other trees in the forest—like the Californian redwood trees that have been able to remain upright for millennia, withstanding the destructive forces of wind, storm, and erosion by growing close together and intermingling and sharing root systems. Prejudice is this tree: The first three conditions are its crown (foliage and branches) and trunk, as it were; the last three its root system. And just as any 'normal' tree will not be gotten rid of by trimming the foliage, cutting the branches, or merely chopping the trunk, unless it be completely deracinated, so prejudice will not be gotten rid of by *reasoning with* it, by endeavoring to defeat it on *rational* grounds, by pointing out that reality is different from what it purports it to be, and by thus aiming to bend its intent. And if it is already hard enough to deracinate a single 'normal' tree, imagine how much harder it must be to uproot a Californian redwood tree, whose very foundation is firmly bound up with the foundations of countless other trees like it. If you can imagine this, you have a pretty good idea of how difficult it is to uproot prejudice. Pulling one or more roots here and there won't do, as the root system as a whole will remain firmly in place and regenerate.[1]

Any given prejudice—to use yet another metaphor that we have used earlier—is a brick firmly cemented into a thick, multi-dimensional wall of prejudice; it is simultaneously imbricated within a system of other prejudices, rooted within a community of hearts and minds, and soldered to a multiplicity of objects. Each member of each string reinforces and supports all the other members in its string, and each string, in turn, reinforces and supports the other two strings. Trying to root out a prejudice, then, is like trying to pull a brick that is firmly cemented into three mutually imbricated walls simultaneously from out of these three walls at the same time. Thus, what makes prejudice so tenacious and enduring is, at bottom, the root system of its three strings—the innermost core of its genetic make-up.

Rarely, if at all, do prejudices disappear. In most cases, when it would seem that a particular prejudice has gone extinct, it will merely lie dormant, ever ready to be reactivated as long as there are enough of those who will validate its six conditions—'those' being mentally competent communities who hold certain kinds of opinions and make certain kinds of judgments about certain other communities although they know that these opinions and judgments are not borne out by facts.

Is this a pessimistic prognosis? Is this to say that I don't truly believe that prejudice can be defeated? And if so, what's the point of this entire discussion of the concept and meaning of 'prejudice'? Does it matter at all, then, whether we know if what someone is voicing is an opinion, conviction, or a prejudice?

I believe it does. Prejudice's hardiness and staying power should not prevent us from aiming at the ideal of rooting it out, for only if we keep our eyes on the ideal and look beyond the horizon of what we already know and know how to do, of what is already within our grasp, will we actually be enjoined—as Robert Browning famously put it—to "reach beyond our grasp" and surpass ourselves. In other words, while counting on the defeat of prejudice might be an implausible and imprudent (if not to say, naïve) stance to take, acting *as if* it were possible is both plausible and prudent; for in so doing, in working toward rooting out prejudice irrespective of whether this enterprise is doomed to failure or not, we will have already done all within our power as *ethical* beings.

In ethical matters, the end is never the goal, the journey is. And in order to undertake this journey successfully, it matters a great deal whether we possess the analytical skills to be able to diagnose prejudice with precision and certainty, and distinguish it from such minor 'illnesses' as being opinionated or having mistaken beliefs.

7

OUTLOOK

~

As I have suggested at the outset of my reflections, once we have understood what makes prejudice so persistent and tenacious, at the level of its DNA, we will also be in a much better position than we have been to determine where and how best to tackle it.

Let us, then, one more time look at the comprehensive definition of prejudice and draw some final conclusions regarding its ethical ramifications. Prejudice has been defined as

> a favorable or unfavorable attitude toward, opinion on, or judgment about someone or something considered as a mere instance or occurrence of a class or type—and thus, by definition, directed at a string of referents—held by a string of proponents of sound mind in spite of sufficient knowledge, information, evidence, experience, or reason not to support or justify such an attitude, opinion, or judgment, carrying an implicit or explicit intent to denigrate, derogate, or detract from someone or something else, and coming with a string of prejudices in tow.

This definition signifies that the following six conditions must be satisfied for an opinion, attitude, or judgment to pass as prejudice: (1) the *sound mind* condition; (2) the *sufficient evidence to the contrary* condition; (3) the *implicit or explicit derogatory intent regarding a third party* condition; (4) the *string of referents* condition; (5) the *string of proponents* condition; (6) the *string of prejudices* condition.

In view of these six positive conditions of prejudice, it is clear under which negative conditions prejudice will not be able to survive: (1) Those who hold prejudice stop being of sound mind; (2) all evidence proving prejudice wrong will somehow be erased; (3) those who hold prejudice will undergo a change of intent; (4) those who suffer the force of prejudice will vanish, and prejudice will have no concrete object; (5) those who hold prejudice will somehow vanish, and prejudice will have no soil to grow in; (6) all individual prejudices will have dissipated.

In order to unhinge prejudice, at least one of its positive conditions needs to be invalidated, or, put differently, at least one of its negative conditions needs to be brought about. Since, clearly, it would be unreasonable, unrealistic, and morally dubious to aim at bringing about negative conditions (1), (2), (4), and (5), we are enjoined, by the very definition of 'prejudice', to home in on the twofold possibility of effecting a change of intent in those who hold prejudice—that is, bringing about negative condition

(3)—and dissipating each individual prejudice—that is, bringing about negative condition (6).

Let us look at the option of rupturing the *string of prejudices* first. Here, two strategies present themselves: targeting each individual prejudice by targeting any given *string of prejudices* in its entirety, or targeting any given *string of prejudices* in its entirety by targeting each prejudice individually. Given that by definition each prejudice is a link in a chain of prejudices—one pearl on a string pearls—tearing the string in one place will suffice to make all other pearls gradually slide off and scatter. Which is to say that it is enough to undo one prejudice to make the entire string crumble.

Interestingly, however, undoing prejudice—the goal of both strategies—cannot, logically speaking, begin by invalidating the *string of prejudices* condition since this would mean, redundantly, aiming at *undoing prejudice by undoing prejudice.* In other words, because the *string of prejudices* condition is the only condition that contains the very term it also helps to define—'prejudice'—its invalidation depends on the invalidation of one of the other five remaining conditions of prejudice. And given that condition (3)—the *implicit or explicit derogatory intent regarding a third party*—can be said to be the *one* condition we can reasonably and realistically aim at invalidating without infracting the parameters set by the moral frameworks within which we operate, we are led to the conclusion that uprooting prejudice ought to begin by tackling prejudicial *intent*.

Let us again remind ourselves why this is the case: (1) Because prejudice is not based on "lack of or insufficient knowledge, information, evidence, [and] experience," *reasoning with* and *teaching* are not the fundamental answers to it. Those who already hold prejudice can be taught to act and speak in ways that don't look or sound prejudicial, but they cannot be taught to stop holding prejudice. You can teach a racist, sexist, or misogynist not to speak and act in racist, sexist, or misogynistic terms—especially, in public—but you cannot *teach* him not to *be* a racist, sexist, or misogynist in his heart and mind. Prejudice will go into hiding, underground, ever ready to be reactivated on a need-to basis. We have all seen this play out in locker room conversations and elsewhere. This, for instance, explains the continued suspicion on the part of some that somewhere in the recesses of their being Germans still harbor the dormant virus of National Socialism, all of the *re-educational* treatments administered to them by the Allied Forces notwithstanding. (2) External force or violence, too, is not the solution to the problem of prejudice.

Thus, we are left with *prejudicial intent* as a point of entry into thinking about concrete ways of efficiently and effectively tackling prejudice. Let us, then, look at prejudicial intent more closely and specify what it is that needs to be achieved step by step for prejudice to be disarmed following the logic of the conditions of prejudice.

One of the essential features of prejudice, I have argued, is an *implicit or explicit intent to denigrate, derogate, or detract from someone or something else.* What this condition of prejudice means is that no prejudice is directed exclusively at one object but in and of itself at more than one, for, as I have explained, the one target it happens to be aiming at in particular is viewed not in its uniqueness but, by definition, in relation to someone or something else, as an instance or occurrence of a class or type. Attempting to disarm prejudice by grabbing hold of this condition, then, means, first and foremost, aiming to take the *third* out of the picture and tear the *string of referents*, or, put positively: It means working toward bringing about a situation in which the object prejudice happens to be directed at is approached and engaged in its uniqueness and not in relation to someone or something else, not merely as an instance or occurrence of a class or type.

Why is this crucial for prejudice to collapse? And what does it actually mean to engage with someone in his very uniqueness?

Let me answer the second question first. Engaging with someone in his very uniqueness means not abstracting from and interpreting him in the light of ready-made theories that we bring to him; it means not from the get-go putting him in his preassigned spot within a grid of meaning, or comparing him with others; it means not treating him as proof of our theory. In positive terms, it means letting the other guide us in our attempts to understand and get to know him rather than making him fit our preconceptions and theories about *people like him*; it means letting the other be the touchstone of our preconceptions and theories; it means changing the latter in light of the former and not the other way around.

This kind of engagement with any given target of prejudice is crucial in the campaign against it because only if we approach the other in his very uniqueness will we be compelled to invalidate the *sufficient evidence to the contrary* condition of prejudice. In other words, only if we actually see what is before us *as it is*, in its very own self-presentation, and not as we think or believe it to be as merely one among a whole range of entities that it may or may not resemble, will we be actually compelled fully to acknowledge the overwhelming evidence against our prejudice.

Let me briefly recap what we have thus far discovered: What needs to be achieved is to make the one holding prejudice against any given object perceive the latter as incomparable and unique, and not as an instance or occurrence of a class or type; for only the concrete uniqueness of the object of prejudice, which, up to now, has been viewed primarily as one among others, as standing in for a type, as merely a bead on a *string of referents*, will carry enough weight to compel the one holding prejudice to pay sufficient attention to what is before him and acknowledge that his prejudice simply doesn't hold up to reality, thereby rupturing the *string of prejudices* that has held all of his individual prejudices in place.

The key question, then, is: How do we reach the point of uniqueness, of experiencing the other in his very uniqueness, as a living, thinking, and acting singularity and not merely as *one* among *many*, which, in turn, is the precondition for allowing our prejudices to founder on the rock of concrete evidence to the contrary?

In order to get to this point—and here we leave the confines of conceptual inquiry and enter the realm of ethics—we need to muster the *courage* to rupture the *string of proponents* at the most basic level of our very *ethos*—our fundamental disposition toward and outlook on the world and others. And it takes courage—a lot of it—to be *different*, to live and think *differently*. For the punishments meted out by those who see themselves and their prejudices exposed by others, who dare to stand out, are severe.

What could possibly be compelling enough to make us decide to muster the courage to be different *and* to brave the daunting task of uprooting our own prejudices. What could be so powerful as to undermine our *prejudicial intent* and sway us into *wanting* to see the *one* instead of the *many*, a unique being instead of a type? Although I have neither a definitive nor a comprehensive answer to this signal question, I believe that the singularizing force of being myself engaged with and treated as a unique being by another will go a long way in compelling me, in turn, to engage with the other in *his* very uniqueness. For uniqueness of this kind is a gift—a gift that comes in the form of an incontrovertible request or injunction, a fundamental *encouragement to become unique* in response to the other's singularizing appeal.

There is no one word to capture this compelling force—'truth', 'love', 'respect', 'friendship' are some of the words that come to mind. It is strongest when it comes from none other than the one at whom prejudice is directed and who must himself show courage that is at least equal to the courage it takes to rupture the *string of proponents* of prejudice in encouraging the one holding prejudice to let go of it. And while the force or incentive compelling us to muster the courage to rupture the *string of proponents* may be strongest when it issues forth from the very victim of prejudice, this should not in any way be taken to imply that the victim of prejudice is responsible for making the one holding prejudice have a change of intent. Neither does it mean that, if the victim of prejudice musters the courage to encourage the one holding prejudice to let go of it, it will also necessarily happen.

~

This is as far as philosophical reflection on the phenomenon of prejudice will take us—to the simple, yet fundamental, realization that disarming and disabling prejudice begins and ends with personal ethics.[1] Only if we succeed in impacting the *ethos* of the one holding prejudice in such a way as to render his prejudices untenable in view of concrete evidence, will other strategies—psychological, educational, socio-cultural, administrative, legal, and political—find a fertile soil in the individual heart and mind to take root in and grow to be more than externally imposed strictures ever in danger of being sabotaged or subverted (more or less tacitly) in the myriad public and private contexts of our personal and professional lives.

How concretely to go about bringing about a change in personal *ethos* is not for me to say—just as it is not for me to tell you how to go about falling in love. The way these things play out in our lives will be different for each of us and in each situation, their potential external similarities notwithstanding. But these things do happen. And when they happen, a window opens onto the possibility of a world with one less prejudice.[2]

GLOSSARY & NOTES

PHILOSOPHICAL GLOSSARY

~

In this glossary, I offer explanations of some of the key terms I use in talking about and defining 'prejudice'. Given that dictionary definitions of all terms are readily available in book form and online, the explanations I provide, while presupposing familiarity with the terms' common acceptions, are of a more personal nature in that they trace my own thinking about them—sometimes in conversation with others, who, I find, have used them in the most interesting and thought-provoking ways.

~

Attitude

'Attitude' is the expression or measure of the angle at which we engage with the world and others, who, in turn, always present themselves to us at a particular angle. 'Attitude' presupposes a certain level of abstraction from 'pure' immediacy—a certain level of self- and other-awareness that exceeds spontaneous engagement with the world around us. Edmund Husserl, the founder of phenomenology, distinguished between two fundamental attitudes that we can assume: the "natural attitude" and the "phenomenological attitude." The former is the attitude we assume as we go about our daily lives and interact with others and the world around us without explicitly and actively reflecting upon it; the latter is the attitude we assume when we mentally take ourselves out of our immediate immersion in whatever it is that we may be engaged in doing and look at it as it *appears* to us—considering it, like a three-dimensional digital image that can be rotated and viewed from every angle and every side, in the virtual reality of our minds. Conceptual thinking is essentially phenomenological.

Bias

It is possible to act in a biased manner without being prejudiced. While prejudice always includes bias, bias doesn't necessarily imply prejudice.

Cliché, Commonplace

Like stereotypes, clichés are impersonal, rhetorical props that can be used for the purpose of general statements. Whereas stereotypes are used in reference to human beings, clichés—like commonplaces—have a broader horizon of reference, pertaining, for instance, to life in general. Thus, 'life is hard' is a cliché, not a 'stereotype'. Neither ought to be confused with 'prejudice'.

Custom, Prevailing Opinion, Tradition

Frequently, these terms are used in the same breath as 'prejudice'. As in the case of 'preconception', it is fair to say that we couldn't live and function without custom, tradition, and prevailing opinion, insofar as, historically speaking, we are always already born into and preceded by them. This, however, does not entail the necessity of prejudice.

Judgment

In logic, a distinction is commonly made between analytic and synthetic judgments. Both kinds of judgment are concerned with the relation between subject and predicate. In the case of analytic judgments, the predicate is considered part of the very concept of the subject; in the case of synthetic judgments, the predicate is considered external to the concept of the subject. From this it follows that analytic judgments are by definition not based on experience, while all judgments of experience are by definition synthetic. Thus, as Immanuel Kant explains in *Critique of Pure Reason*, "all bodies are extended" is an analytic judgment because the very concept of 'body' implies extension, whereas "all bodies are heavy" is a synthetic judgment because the concept of 'body' does not imply 'being heavy'—this, according to Kant, can only be known from experience. In light of the distinction between synthetic and analytic judgments, 'prejudice' could be described as a false synthetic judgment posing as an analytic judgment.

Opinion

In his dialogue *Theatetus* (189e), Plato defines thinking as the "soul's dialogue with itself." When the soul thinks, Socrates explains to Theatetus, it is "merely conversing with itself, asking itself questions and answering, affirming and denying." When it arrives at a "decision … and is at last agreed and is not in doubt," Socrates continues, "we call it its opinion." Based on this notion of thinking as inner dialogue, 'opinion' is defined as "talk that has been held not with someone else, nor yet aloud, but in silence with oneself."

In *The Sophist* (263e-264b), Plato reiterates that "opinion is the final result of thought," defined as "the soul's dialogue with itself," and makes the additional point that, since opinion is essentially a form of speech and since speech can be true or false, "opinion," too, can "sometimes be false." Thus, 'opinion' is very close to judgment in that it implies that a statement or proposition is being made about the world.

Unlike prejudice, an opinion can be held by one person only and refer to a single object (person, state of affairs, thing etc.); moreover, it doesn't actively have to summon other opinions or be negative.

Preconception, Preconceived Idea

These and other similar terms must be distinguished from 'prejudice' since they signify the state of not having sufficient knowledge, information, data etc. regarding any given object. Because they have been used interchangeably with 'prejudice', it has been (falsely) legitimate to claim that we cannot live and function without prejudice, for it is true to say that we cannot live and function without preconceptions, preconceived ideas, and opinions (see *Custom*).

Stereotype

'Stereotype' is often used virtually interchangeably with 'prejudice', as in: 'racial prejudice' or 'racial stereotyping'. As I have explained, however, 'stereotype' should be clearly distinguished from 'prejudice'. For instance, unlike 'prejudice', 'stereotype' can be positive (truly favorable) as well as negative, and it doesn't have to be based on an intent to denigrate, derogate or detract from someone or something.

More importantly, unlike 'prejudice', 'stereotype' doesn't imply *active* will and *live* intent. What does this mean? It means that while prejudice only lives if there are actual people who actually hold it, who actually harbor an intent to denigrate etc., stereotypes are 'out there', like so many differently colored glasses neatly arranged in the store rooms of our culture, ready to be put on on a need-to basis. In other words, live prejudice implies a certain performative thrust here and now. This is not to say that the other five conditions of prejudice—the *sound mind* condition, the *sufficient evidence to the contrary* condition, the *string of referents* condition, the *string of proponents* condition, and the *string of prejudices* condition—would somehow be subordinated to the *implicit or explicit derogatory intent regarding a third party* condition; it merely means that like the heart in the human body, which is only one among a number of necessary items that make a living body, derogatory intent injects all other conditions, on which its functioning in turn depends, with movement and direction.

Even a 'dead' prejudice—a prejudice that is no longer held by an individual or a community and is merely remembered as having once been held—does not turn into a stereotype, although there are stereotypes that look like dead prejudices.

NOTES

~

CHAPTER 1: THE PERSISTENCE OF PREJUDICE

1. For scholarly-scientific approaches to the study of prejudice, I refer the reader in particular to Gordon W. Allport's classical 1954 study *The Nature of Prejudice*, Elisabeth Young-Bruehl's compendious *The Anatomy of Prejudice* (Cambridge: Harvard University Press, 1996), Timothy D. Wilson's *Strangers to Ourselves: Discovering the Adaptive Unconscious* (Cambridge: Harvard University Press, 2002), and Jens Förster's *Brief Introduction to Cookie-Cutter Thinking: On the Advantages and Disadvantages of Prejudice (Kleine Einführung ins Schubladendenken: Über Nutzen und Nachteil des Vorurteils)* (Munich: DVA, 2007).

2. As Timothy D. Wilson writes in *Strangers to Ourselves: Discovering the Adaptive Unconscious*: "... prejudice persists ... It is not hard to find ... signs of continuing prejudice" (pp. 188-189). For insightful studies on the continuous prevalence of prejudice, I refer the reader in particular to Mark Buchanan's *The Social Atom: Why the Rich Get Richer, Cheaters Get Caught, and Your Neighbor Usually Looks Like You* (New York: Bloomsbury, 2007) and Farhad Manjoo's *True Enough: Learning to Live in a Post-Fact Society* (Hoboken: John Wiley & Sons, 2008). Relying on the work of political scientists Robert Axelrod and Ross Hammond, who suggest that prejudices "help us cooperate," Buchanan observes that with the

growth of the "overall level of cooperation in this world ... people become more prejudiced" as well (pp. 144, 151). Manjoo, in turn, documents in great detail how the cognitive and informational fragmentation of the contemporary world due to the virtually boundless proliferation of media and news outlets makes for a "landscape [that] will also, inevitably, help us to indulge our biases and preexisting beliefs" (p. 17). More than ever, Manjoo argues, we are able to avoid cognitive dissonance through selective exposure to those who will reinforce our prejudices.

CHAPTER 2: THE 'PICKLER INCIDENT'

1. *17 Prejudices That We Germans Hold Against America and Americans and That Can't Quite Be True* was published in German under the pseudonym Misha Waiman. The original title is *17 Vorurteile, die wir Deutschen gegen Amerika und die Amerikaner haben und die so nicht ganz stimmen können* (New York: Upper West Side Philosophers, Inc., 2008).

2. Kelly Pickler was a guest on *Are You Smarter Than a 5th Grader* on November 15, 2007. The YouTube clip of her performance can be found at: http://www.youtube.com/watch? v=ANTDkfkoBaI.

3. William Hazlitt's (1778-1830) quip can be found in his essay "On Prejudice" (cited in *Sketches and Essays* [London: John Templeman, 1839], p. 98). The classical modern formulation of the pro-prejudice doctrine can be found in Edmund Burke's (1729-1797) *Reflections on*

the Revolution in France (edited by J. G. Pocock. Indianapolis: Hackett, 1987, pp. 76-77):

> ... instead of casting away all our old prejudices, we cherish them to a very considerable degree ... because they are prejudices, and the longer they have lasted and the more generally they have prevailed, the more we cherish them. We are afraid to put men to live and trade on their own private stock of reason, because we suspect that this stock in each man is small, and that the individuals would do better to avail themselves of the general bank and capital of nations and of ages ... Prejudice is of ready application in the emergency; it previously engages the mind in a steady course [and] does not leave the man hesitating in the moment of decision skeptical, puzzled, and unresolved.

Many a follower has since rallied around Burke's pro-prejudice battle cry, including William Hazlitt, Hans-Georg Gadamer (1900-2002)—whose project of "rehabilitating" the "authority" of prejudice as purveyor of "tradition" and "source of truth" became hugely influential in the latter half of the last century (see Gadamer's 1960 book *Truth and Method*, Part II, 2, 1[B])—and, most recently, Theodore Dalrymple, in his 2007 book *In Praise of Prejudice: The Necessity of Preconceived Ideas* (New York: Encounter Books).

At the other end, we have Socrates—the epitome of a life devoted precisely to the pursuit of his "own private stock of reason" in the face of false opinion—

and *his* seminal modern followers: René Descartes, Immanuel Kant, John Stuart Mill, and Edmund Husserl, all of whom have mounted massive attacks against the "general bank and capital of nations and of ages" in the name of independent thinking. Poignantly, and in stark opposition to Gadamer's rehabilitation project, German-Jewish philosopher Edmund Husserl (1859-1938) wrote on the eve of the Holocaust: "Thinking for yourself, being an autonomous thinker with a will to liberate yourself from all prejudices demands that you realize that everything you take for granted is prejudice and that all prejudices are obscurities arising out of a sedimentation of tradition and not merely judgments whose truth is yet undecided …" (*The Crisis of European Sciences and Transcendental Phenomenology*, §15).

4. "The world is all that is the case" is the first proposition of Ludwig Wittgenstein's groundbreaking *Tractatus Logico-Philosophicus*, published in 1921.

5. Pertinently, in *Strangers to Ourselves: Discovering the Adaptive Unconscious*, Timothy D. Wilson observes: "… stereotyping is probably innate, we are prewired to fit people into categories" (p. 53).

6. Theodore Dalrymple's *In Praise of Prejudice: The Necessity of Preconceived Ideas* is an exemplary case of such terminological confusion. Dalrymple uses 'prejudice' indiscriminately to mean: "likes and dislikes"; "habit"; "custom, law, wisdom of the ages"; "attitude"; "prevailing opinion"; "received opinion"; "tradition"; "preexisting authority"; "predisposition, … presupposition, and propensity" (pp. 7, 20-21, 44, 55, 59, 87, 122).

CHAPTER 3: WHAT IS & WHAT IS NOT PREJUDICE

1. The term 'prejudice' originated in Roman law, where it primarily referred to legal action devoted to fact-finding and preceding actual judgment: "A *praeiudicium* is an *actio*, which has not any *condemnatio* as a consequence but only a judicial declaration as to the existence of a legal relation. The name of this kind of actions comes from the circumstance that they serve as preliminary to other and future actions." (*Dictionary of Greek and Roman Antiquities*, p. 954; cited on www.ancientlibrary.com). *Praeiudicium* was also used in the sense of "inconvenience, damage, injury" in Roman law, which appears to have arisen from the "notion of a thing being prejudged or decided without being fairly heard; and this sense of the word seems to be very nearly the same in which it occurs in our law in the phrase 'without prejudice to other matters in the cause'" (ibid.).

2. We may be "prewired," as Timothy Wilson has argued, to "fit people into categories," but this doesn't mean that we are prewired to hold prejudice. In his 2008 book *Proust Was a Neuroscientist* (Boston: Houghton Mifflin, p. 70), Jonah Lehrer makes an interesting additional point, suggesting that "[o]ur human brain" is "wired so that prejudices *feel* like facts" (my emphasis).

3. *The New York Times* "Personal Business" section of December 29, 2007, features a story by the wine critic Harry Hurt III, who conducted blind taste tests to determine the validity of our "oenological opinions." On one occasion he served his two test subjects—

Gisela and Gaston—a variety of Champagne-like beverages that included a number of fairly cheap sparkling wines, such as a "Boyer Brut for $9.95" and one real Champagne, a "$65 Veuve Cliquot Rosé." "The real shocker," Harry Hurt remembers, "was the Veuve Cliquot Rosé ... Gaston erroneously insisted that it was 'definitely not Champagne' ... Gisela was even more disparaging. 'This one is kind of girlie, like a California rosé,' she declared. 'It tastes like some cheesy seduction number a guy would try to pass off on me for Valentine's Day'." "The rose-colored tint of the Veuve Cliquot," Hurt concludes, "paled in comparison to the red that flushed the faces on my taste testers when I revealed its true identity. Learning the identities of the other eight bottles prompted similar embarrassments. But by that point, Gisela and Gaston were feeling no pain and neither was I. We poured three measures of the Boyer Brut, our consensus favorite, and raised our flutes ..." Clearly, Gisela and Gaston allowed themselves to stand corrected in their preconceptions about the presumably intrinsic qualities of Champagne, thus not giving into prejudice. Had they continued to insist on the superiority of Champagne to other kinds of sparkling wine simply because it is Champagne, however, it would be fair to call them prejudiced.

Prejudice proper can thus be said to set in only *after* we have been alerted to and given the chance to 'overcome' what behavioral economist Dan Arieli has recently diagnosed as our day-to-day "predictable irrationality" (*Predictably Irrational: The Hidden Forces That Shape Our Decisions* [New York: HarperCollins, 2008]).

Already Gordon W. Allport, the pioneer of contemporary prejudice studies, pointed out that "prejudgments become prejudices only if they are not reversible when exposed to new knowledge" (*The Nature of Prejudice*, 25th Anniversary edn. [New York: Basic Books, 1979], p. 9). Allport's point has recently been reiterated by Carol Tavris and Elliot Aronson in their 2007 book *Mistakes Were Made (But Not By Me): Why We Justify Foolish Beliefs, Bad Decisions, and Hurtful Acts* (Orlando: Harcourt, Inc.). The "hallmark of prejudice," Tavris and Aronson write, "is that it is impervious to reason, experience, and counterexample" (p. 60).

Interestingly, by and large, Allport's observation that prejudice is predicated on its proponents' awareness that it is rationally and empirically untenable seems to have fallen by the wayside even in scholarly treatments of the topic (including Allport's own). Thus, in his recent book *Brief Introduction to Cookie-Cutter Thinking: On the Advantages and Disadvantages of Prejudice*, sociologist Jens Förster defines prejudice as a "judgment based on a preconceived opinion about a member of a group that we don't know enough about" (p. 21). In light of Allport's initial insight into the cognitive structure of prejudice, the viability of the popular notion of "unconscious" or "nonconscious" prejudice must seriously be doubted. For scholarly and popular discussions of "unconscious prejudice" (a term coined by W. B. Carpenter in his 1874 book *Principles in Mental Psychology*), I refer the reader in particular to Timothy D. Wilson's *Strangers To Ourselves: Discovering the Adaptive Unconscious* (esp., pp. 183-194) and Malcolm Gladwell's *Blink: The*

Power of Thinking Without Thinking (New York: Little, Brown, and Company, 2005, pp. 78-88).

4. Interestingly, even the official definition of 'prejudice' by the American Psychological Association as a "learned attitude toward a target object, involving negative affect (dislike or fear), negative beliefs (stereotypes) that justify the attitude, and a behavioral intention to avoid, control, dominate, or eliminate the target object," omits prejudice's directedness at someone or something else in addition to its immediate object (see www.psychologymatters.org/glossary.html).

CHAPTER 4: THE STRING THEORY OF PREJUDICE

1. In his groundbreaking 1917 book *On the Nature and Forms of Sympathy*, German ethical philosopher Max Scheler suggests that "'anti-Semitism', 'anti-Germanism', 'anti-Frenchism', etc. can go hand in hand with loving an individual Jew, German, or French person" (Part B, 1, 1). I am not sure how this could be possible, unless we radically redefine the concept of 'love' to include an aspect of fundamental hostility toward core constituents of the beloved's very identity.

2. See my *17 Prejudices That We Germans Hold Against America and Americans and That Can't Quite Be True*, pp. 15-53.

3. The irony of this common perception of Germans is all the more striking given that Germany is apparently nowhere near the top on the list of cultures and countries most prone to what Dutch psychologist

Geert Hofstede has called "uncertainty avoidance"—that is, as Malcolm Gladwell explains, "most reliant on rules and plans and most likely to stick to procedure regardless of circumstances" (*Outliers: The Story of Success* [New York: Little, Brown and Company, 2008], p. 203). Surprisingly, as Gladwell points out, the "top five 'uncertainty avoidance' countries [are]: 1. Greece; 2. Portugal; 3. Guatemala; 4. Uruguay; 5. Belgium" (ibid.).

CHAPTER 6: THE TENACITY OF PREJUDICE

1. I should emphasize that in no way am I advocating the destruction of the California redwoods, which merely serve as a metaphor here on account of their unique, intermingling root systems. The ideal image would be one of weeds with intermingling root systems.

CHAPTER 7: OUTLOOK

1. Gordon W. Allport's observation that "perhaps the best of all methods for changing [prejudicial] attitudes is under conditions of individual psychotherapy" (*The Nature of Prejudice*, p. 495) makes perfect sense in light of the DNA of prejudice and the ethical course of 'treatment' enjoined it.

2. In his 2005 book *Blink: The Power of Thinking Without Thinking* (pp. 245-248, 254), Malcolm Gladwell relates two anecdotes that poignantly capture the hold

prejudice has on us on the one hand, and, on the other hand, the beauty of those moments when the walls of prejudice crumble under the weight of personal uniqueness. (Although Gladwell is not concerned with 'uniqueness' so much as with what he calls "Blink moments"—moments when we "think without thinking"—these two anecdotes palpably illustrate my point about the role of uniqueness in any attempt at disarming prejudice.)

The first anecdote is about world-class trombonist Abbie Conant, who, in 1980, applied and was invited to audition for the first trombone position with the Munich Philharmonic Orchestra. Ominously, the invitation letter was addressed to "Mr. Abbie Conant." After Conant had finished her blind audition, the Philharmonic's illustrious music director, Sergiu Celibidache, cried out, ""That's who we want!"" When Conant stepped out from behind the screen, however, she was greeted with a gasp of disbelief and dismay on the part of the members of the hiring committee. As the invitation letter had suggested, the committee was expecting a man. "Once Celibidache and the rest of the selection committee saw her in the flesh," Gladwell observes, "all those long-held prejudices began to compete with the winning first impressions they had of her performance." Although Conant was hired to play first trombone, she was soon demoted to second trombone —"We need a man for the solo trombone," she was told. Conant spent her remaining thirteen years in Munich locked in a protracted court battle with the Philharmonic. "Sergiu Celibidache, the man complaining about her [Conant's] ability," Gladwell wistfully concludes, "had listened to her play ... and in that unbiased moment, he had said, 'That's who we want!' ..." (Gladwell's retelling of Abbie Conant's story is based on William Osborne's award-winning account of his wife's experiences in the male-dominated world of professional classical music, entitled "You Sound Like A Ladies' Orchestra" [http://www.osborne-conant.org/ladies.htm]).

The second anecdote is about Julie Landsman, principal French horn player at the Metropolitan Opera in New York. Like Abbie Conant, Landsman auditioned for the position at a time when "everyone 'knew' that women could not play the horn [or the trombone] as well as men." Like Conant's, Landsman's audition was blind; like Conant, Landsman was declared the winner; and like Conant, Landsman, too, was greeted with a "gasp" when she "stepped out from behind the screen ..." This is where the parallels between Conant's and Landsman's stories end, however: In Landsman's case, the selection committee members' gasp wasn't due to the fact that she was not a man so much as that "they knew her," for she "had played for the Met before as a substitute." Remarkably, Gladwell muses, until "they listened to her with just their ears ... they had no idea she was so good." Now, however, "they saw her for who she truly was"—in her uniqueness.

ACKNOWLEDGMENTS

~

No thinking happens in a vacuum, and neither did mine. And while I am solely responsible for the contents of this book, I am profoundly grateful to all those who have listened to me and given me feedback over the years in private and in public—during readings, lectures, and workshops—thus helping me to develop, test, and adjust my thinking about prejudice without losing sight of the actual phenomenon of prejudice as we encounter it in everyday life.

In particular, I would like to thank Matthew G. Boyse, Bernd Herbert, Franz Klug, Kathrin DiPaola, Frederick A. Lubich, Robert Kohen, Elias and Benno Stengel-Eskin, Susan Winnett, and Jeffrey Rothfeder. Last but not least, I would like to thank Jean-Paul Schmetz, Licia Carlson, and Kathrin Stengel, without whose pointed queries, detailed criticisms, powerful objections, and creative suggestions this would be a very different book; I am fortunate to have had the three of them as my *advocati diaboli*.

ABOUT THE AUTHOR

~

Michael Eskin was educated at the University of Munich, the Institut Catholique de Paris, Concordia College, and Rutgers University. A former fellow of Sidney Sussex College, Cambridge, he has taught at the University of Cambridge and at Columbia University. He has published widely on philosophical, cultural, and literary subjects, including: *Nabokov's Version of Pushkin's "Eugene Onegin": Between Version and Fiction—a Study in Translation and Fiction Theory* (Sagner, 1994); *Ethics and Dialogue in the Works of Levinas, Bakhtin, Mandel'shtam, and Celan* (Oxford University Press, 2000); *Literature and Ethics: A Special Edition of Poetics Today* (Duke University Press, 2004); *Poetic Affairs: Celan, Grünbein, Brodsky* (Stanford University Press, 2008); *17 Prejudices That We Germans Hold Against America and Americans and That Can't Quite Be True* (UWSP, 2008; published in German under the pseudonym 'Misha Waiman'); *Philosophical Fragments of a Contemporary Life* (UWSP, 2008; under the pseudonym 'Julien David'); *The Bars of Atlantis: Selected Essays by Durs Grünbein* (as editor, Farrar, Straus and Giroux, 2010). Michael Eskin lectures regularly across the United States and Europe on subjects as diverse as poetry, philosophy, and cultural and ethnic prejudice—most recently, as a guest of the

United States Consulate General, Germany, the Federation of German-American Clubs, and Limmud, an international organization fostering cross-cultural Jewish education. He lives in New York City with his wife and three sons.